Praise For

"Wrap It Up!"©
The Guy's Guide
to Giving & Gifts

What a gift you are giving by writing this book! I consider myself a caring, giving and romantic person, but your book puts all of this at another level. You are going to improve a lot of lives with this book. I can't wait to start checking off your ideas as I use them.

Terry Crowther
Vision Coach
Married to an Angel

My U.S. Senator dad always complained about the frustrations of buying gifts for the women in his life. I've bought a dozen copies of *"Wrap It Up!"*'s so every man in our family can have one of his own. There will be a lot of happy faces from now on.

Peggy Goldwater Clay

If I'd had Ann Crowell's *"Wrap It Up!"* when I was in the dating pool, life would have been so much easier. This funny and unique guide is the answer to making relationships run smoothly. Thanks Ann for helping us become mind readers.

Skip Jenings
Motivation To Change Your Life
Speaker, Trainer

This book does more than just teach us men how to buy gifts for all the important ladies in our lives. It gives us peace-of-mind and easy methods to insure we get the perfect gift. This new tool will ultimately lead to a better expression of appreciation—in both directions.

Heath Celestin
Image Consultant
For Men

Other Books By Ann Hult Crowell

Ann Hult Crowell
*The Ad Agent © — How to Make Big Budget Marketing
Strategies Work for Small Budget Success*

Crowell McKay, 1981

Ann Hult Crowell & Ann Coil. Ph.D.
The Career Portfolio®, Standard Edition

DayTimer®, 2000

Ann Hult Crowell & Ann Coil. Ph.D.
The Career Portfolio®, College Edition

DayTimer®, 2000

Ann Hult Crowell & Ann Coil. Ph.D.
*Performance Reviews / Empowered Careers — Powerful
Communications That Advance Careers*

Impact Publishing, 2002

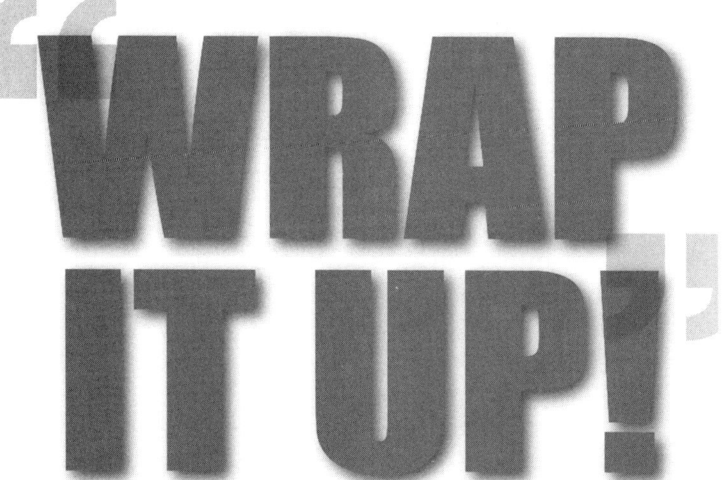

"WRAP IT UP!"

The Guy's Guide to Giving & Gifts

Ann Hult Crowell

B.I.G. Publishing

Laguna Beach, California

Cover Design and Illustrations by
David Haight Design

Printed in the United States of America
by Sheridan Books, Inc.

ISBN 0-9773454-0-8

Dedication

To my mother,
Betty Hult McKay,
the inspiration behind
all my best choices, and
my father, Stanley Earl Hult, who
taught me about the priceless gifts
money can't buy.

Contents

Author's Preface

My guiding principal for this book was born out of respect for your manly preferences that it be:

"Short, useful and to the point."

To that end, I abandoned our female hard wiring that requires we use thousands of words — as you know— where a few would do quite nicely.

As a result, you'll find:

- Short and useful lists at the <u>front of every chapter</u> plus helpful hints and how-to's spiced with wisdom and humor to keep you entertained and informed.
- *Outta Sight Insights©* that reveal a few feminine secrets that may aid in your pursuits.
- A peek into our perplexing and unpredictable behavior — without destroying the mystery.
- Plus, new ways you can express your adoration and uncover what really makes us glow. Yes! Even in the dark.

We make a living by what we get,
but we make a life by what we give.

Winston Churchill

Introduction

A Personal Letter From The Author

Okay you guys, gentlemen and young-men-at-heart, I know about you. And I know what you're looking for out of this book.

"Rewards." Right? Because, face it, all you shining knights, with or without armor have sought rewards.

It's what knights also expect for their loyal and loving efforts in the illusive quest for love. After all, you're battling for the attentions of the object-of-your-affection — against worthy competitors — and you want to win.

"Wrap It Up!"© is your secret weapon to make you appealing above all others and to put you first in line for the gratitude and delectable and memorable rewards that we, your affection-objects, are well able to deliver. As you like it.

Wait a minute, though, you have a part in this. A big part. Often subtle, but necessary to achieve your objective.

Take note that *"Wrap It Up!"* isn't about the "gift," it's about the "giving." And therein lies the rub.

The journey can be enthralling, redolent with indescribable sensations when you least expect them and that you can't forget afterwards.

It can also be a personal challenge — calling out of you the man who's been restrained inside. The man you may not have acknowledged existed until now.

You may discover a fierce inner battle over which one of you will be there in the end for her. Scary stuff for you heroes. You men of action. Men of our dreams.

No fears though. The winning strategy is simple and fulfilling:

> "Let your heart call the shots and
> you win every time."

It's NOT the most handsome, smartest, finest of physical specimens or wallet size that captures our hearts. It's your True Self we're seeking and that's who wins our devotion every time. Guaranteed!

Go ahead. Slay the dragon. Remove the chains that imprison your true feelings and let us see the "real" man you are. The one you may have kept in hiding. Then ponder the abundant rewards that await.

"Wrap It Up!" is ready to deliver the help you need and to celebrate the joy you'll experience from giving.

"Wrap It Up!" is the map to enriching all your relationships — work, play or romantic. It's your personal guide to ever-expanding joy and happiness.

Go forward, men, and remember to enjoy every exhilarating, heart-throbbing moment along the way.

The intuitive mind is a sacred gift and
the rational mind is a faithful servant.
We have created a society
that honors the servant
and has forgotten the gift.

Albert Einstein

The 7 Secrets Of Highly Successful Givers

1. The gifts are on time
    Successful Givers (SGs) use repeated reminders
    to be on time 24/7/365

2. The gifts are thoughtful
    SGs listen and observe. Record their findings,
    and take action accordingly

3. They fit
    SGs are familiar with the Recipient's personality,
    preferences and body size

4. Gifts represent an investment of time
    SGs understand it's the effort that counts!

5. Recipients don't have to pick out their
    gifts for the SG

6. SGs give many priceless gifts that don't
    cost a penny
    SGs know this is where <u>frequency really counts</u>

7. The Gift and Giver are both well *packaged*
    for the presentation

Why Give Gifts?

By the time you get to the end of *"Wrap It Up!"* you'll have everything you want and need to know to delight someone.

The buying and giving of gifts will become a pleasurable, stress-free experience for you and your recipients whether they're personal, work or family.

"Wrap It Up!" makes it SO SIMPLE and gratifying. It delivers everything you need to transform your life from so-so to sublime.

It's all here, and it's entertaining reading. Full of easy to find gifts that bring mutual pleasure for both of you. Plus the heartwarming experiences you've been seeking.

Lick your chops, gentlemen, and stay tuned. You'll have the "giving thing" wired in no time and start smiling very soon. And a lot. For as along as you live. You'll discover that the cost of the gift will become irrelevant. After all, it's not about the "gift," it's about the "giving." And giving is something you can do with fanfare — <u>without spending a penny</u>. See Chapter Nine.

For those who are wired to business 24/7 and barely have time for a conversation with the Object-Of-Your-Affection, much less remembering dates, figuring out what-in-the-world-she-wants, where to get it etc., consider this:

> Next time you're stuck in traffic or getting antsy in the ATM line, treat yourself to a mental break and fantasize about all the loving responses you'll receive from your Special Other.

Then grab *"Wrap It Up!"* and your *Pocket Informant©* (wallet-size reference guide, see last chapter for details), now plot your next move and take action.

You have no idea what you've been missing all this time. I know, because you've told me about gift-buying stress and that you need help! NOW.

With *"Wrap It Up!"* you have the answers. Plus simple strategies you can use now and experience loving and tasty benefits that are lying in wait for you — you deserving man.

The great question . . .
which I have not been able to answer,
despite my thirty years of research
into the feminine soul is,
"What does a woman want?"

Sigmund Freud

"What <u>Does</u> A Woman Want?"

Sigmund,
Here's a thought in response to your question. Let me know what you think. Thank you.

Ann

1. <u>People say, "Honey, just surprise me — please!"</u>

You and I both know that's <u>not</u> an answer to your question, and is totally insensitive and unfair. I have a solution. All wrapped up here in *"Wrap It Up!"*

2. <u>What most recipients want and *never* ask for is: "More of you. Your time. Your love. Your affec- tion. To know that you cherish me."</u>

We both like research and documented findings, which are the basis for *"Wrap It Up!"* Its purpose is to answer, "What Does A Woman Want?" and men's other urgent questions about giving and gifts.

Getting To Know
Their Favorite Things

1. **Their likes:**
    Golf, hiking, biking, skiing, tennis, driving trips, desert, mountains, beach, conversation, books, high risk sports, etc.

2. **Their favorite things:**
    Color, flower, author, song, magazine, music

3. **Their favorite food:**
    Sushi, meat and potatoes, ice cream

4. **Their favorite restaurants:**
    For candlelight dinners, quick nourishment, casual, small, quaint, intimate, glitzy, grandiose, romantic, cozy at home

5. **Their favorite entertainment:**
    Movies, plays, museums, galleries, actors, musicians, places to walk and hold hands, sightsee, play miniature golf, etc.

6. **Their favorite (or aversion to) animals:**
    Cats — Dander
    Dogs — Barking, exercise demands
    Birds — Cleaning cages, early AM chirping

10 Important Things
To Remember

1. The date. The date. The date. THE DATE!

2. Plan ahead

3. Wrap the gift (Chapter Seven)

4. Enclose a card. From a card shop, the car wash or supermarket. A plain piece of paper with your hand-written message inside

5. A card alone can be the gift — *unless* the occasion is One of the 8 Biggies (Chapter Three)

6. The most "priceless gifts" which don't cost a penny

7. Keep the receipts

8. No gifts involving batteries

9. Diamonds are a girl's best friend

10. Always keep breath mints in your pocket

Stop!

Look!

And Listen!

Outta Sight Insights©
Discover What Makes Us Tick.

We Recipients Drop Lots Of Gift Hints.
All Year Long.

Sometimes they're soooo obvious. Talking with my friends — just like your recipients — it's amazing how these clear-as-a-bell, bold hints slip by you totally unnoticed and fall through the cracks. We're dumbfounded!

"Huh?" we say. How <u>do you manage to miss our barrage of hints</u>? We always end up with, "... we love you and figure it's a guy thing."

I have a theory about why you miss these hints. First, current academic research has confirmed that women say about 17,000 words a day, whereas you gentlemen speak only 5,000.
No surprise to you — right?

My sense is that the moment you men hear "word noises" from her side of the car or couch, you tune out until you hear something like, "What do you think about that?" And you sheepishly ask, "About what again?" Who could blame you? Right?

Suffice to say this "hearing" is just not in your DNA. And that's okay. However, now that you understand each other, how would it be for you to do a couple of little things that can benefit both of you? Try this:

LISTEN — ON PURPOSE — BRIEFLY when "word noise" is launched. You'll know in a sentence or two where the words are headed. They'll probably be going in one of three directions.

1. You'll be receiving driving or other *valuable* instructions of some sort.

2. It will be continued commentary about some of your shortcomings. We have you trapped in the car, so it's a good time — as we see it — to present some issues you escape hearing about at home. (Oops. Did I say that?)

3. We take off on a lengthy diatribe about a topic that is NOT mutually interesting. In which case you can quietly tune out. I'll never tell.
   PSST: Just hope there's no "pop quiz" at the end.

When you DO hear an expression of an idea or preference about something we like to eat, wear, or saw recently in a shop or magazine, know THIS IS A "HINT." TAKE CLEAR MENTAL NOTE. Write it down ASAP in your *Pocket Informant©*.

Next time your recipient unwraps your gift, they'll know it was your sensitive insight at work and will say something like, "How ever did you know?" Just smile and relax. Wait a minute and see how this listening pays off — in "Rewards" back to you!

They'll <u>know you listened</u> and trust me, will be thrilled. They'll make every attempt to show you just how thrilled they are.

<u>Never</u> give utilitarian housewares,
cleaning equipment or
chore-related items.
If you're on a budget and
need it now — BUY it.
DON'T make it 'The Gift.' EVER.

Cleo Brynmar

Educator, Author, Speaker

Chapter
Three

THE 8 MUST-GIVE-A-GIFT EVENTS

Blow It Here And You're *Toast!*

1. Birthday

2. Anniversary

3. Major Holidays

4. Valentine's Day

5. Mother's Day

6. Father's Day

7. Your Own "Special Day"

8. The Kiss-And-Make-Up Gift

The Top Ten Classic Gifts

1. Flowers
2. Perfume
3. Jewelry
4. Champagne
5. Chocolate
6. Lingerie
7. Dinner
8. Music
9. Theater Performance
10. Art

Two Top Cop-Outs	**Possible Exceptions**
1. A Gift Certificate	Enough for a *Special Item* at her favorite shop
2. Cash In An Envelope	Attention-getting *Cold Cash (See pg. 118)*

A True Kiss-And-Make-Up Story

The Burns (George Burns and Gracie Allen) were always praised as having one of the happiest marriages in show business. Friends said that they were to marriage what Rogers and Hammerstein were to music-style, dignity and class all the way.

Burns later admitted that on one occasion he had an affair with a Las Vegas showgirl. He said it was the biggest regret of his life. Although Gracie found out about it and he knew she had, they never discussed it.

Burns felt so bad that to make amends he bought his wife a diamond ring and a mink coat.

Sometime later, Gracie was shopping with a friend and said "You know I really wish George would cheat on me again. I really like that diamond ring and mink coat."

Unless your indiscretion suggests that a mink coat and a diamond ring are in order — think Kobe Bryant — there are plenty of pleasing alternatives that reinforce your love and caring without tainting the mega-gift that you would prefer to give on a birthday or anniversary.

Read *Outta Sight Insights©*, For Gift Ideas And To Uncover New Ways To Celebrate on the next page.

PSST VIP:

Again, if kiss-and-make-up gifts are a <u>repeat</u> event, do yourself and others a favor. Consider therapy, an anger management program or AA (and Al-Anon for your significant other) and stick with it. More rich and loving moments and a much happier life lie ahead.

Outta Sight Insights©
Uncover New Ways To Celebrate

**Inspired Ideas To Get Your
"8 Big Event"
Creative Juices Flowing
And Stop The *Stress*
Before It Starts!!!**

1. Birthdays

All birthdays are important.
Landmark birthdays are on-the-top-of-the-list and important because they're also milestones that deserve fanfare.

Recipients include wife, significant other, mother, dad, children, #1 girlfriend or best friend. When in doubt, err on the side of generosity.

Early Birthdays
>The 5th is the best. It represents Kindergarten.
>>School bus. Big beginnings.
>>>How about a "cool" lunch box or
>>>book bag to carry on the bus

First Double-Digit Birthday

Have a party for 10 friends.

Instead of cake do 10 decorated cupcakes with a candle on each

Go play miniature golf

Arrange a snowman contest

Play 10 games with prizes so everyone can win

The Teen Arrives

The transition into adulthood. You ready?

- Bat and Bas Mitzvah's or other events
- A party where guests can come dressed like their favorite movie or music star — they have to perform.

Sweet 16 and Quincinera Celebrations

Very special attention required.

- Make it special. Keep it sane.
- A lot of young people have "great expectations" for this event. "Budget-straining expectations." If your budget is restrained, get creative and do something very special for a select few — like just family or a few close friends, too. Don't overlook Surprise Breakfast parties. Or a dress-up fancy dinner for a few friends, in a <u>limousine</u>.

The 21st. Hold Your Breath
This is *their* event.
- Arrange a surprise gathering for his/her friends at *their* favorite eatery. For their best friends.
- You show up for the "surprise" part only, then disappear.
- If you're serving alcohol, state a budget and/or drinks limit and hope someone sober drives. Best idea: hire a Limo. This is no time for sad endings.
- Do a special family party another night.

39 Again! <u>Pay Close Attention</u>
Test the waters about age-related *public* announcements, and then decide how to proceed.
- Dinner at the Honoree's favorite place
- Keep it a secret
- A special table
- Champagne waiting
- Friends, too?
- YOU arrange the sitter
- Tell her the appropriate dress or call her girlfriend for how-to-dress help

We'll help you remember The Dates FREE!
Go to *www.wrapitupbooks.com* and click on My Giving Guide.

2. Anniversaries

Good time to ignite your creativity. Brainstorm with a friend, a seasoned giving sage or an experienced recipient.

- Buy her a generous gift. Have it wrapped.
- Get flowers delivered to her early in the day at work or at home in the afternoon, or buy a bunch on your way home from the office
- Plan a "Honeymoon Weekend" away
- Put a card on her pillow, on her windshield
- Hire a limo for a special dinner out

Buy a traditional gift:

Anniversary	Gift
1st	Paper
2nd	Cotton
3rd	Leather
4th	Flowers
5th	Wood
10th	Tin
15th	Crystal
20th	China
25th	Silver
30th	Pearl
40th	Ruby
50th	Gold
60th	Diamond
70th	Emeralds

You're also welcome to ignore tradition and give anything her heart may desire or yours wants her to
have.

Something from Tiffany in their robins egg blue box
tied in white ribbon is always a fine choice. Happily,
they have truly affordable items as well as those that
make headlines in movie star magazines.

JUST REMEMBER THE:
     DATE
     GIFT
     CARD
     KISS

Good night and good luck.

Edward R. Murrow

To assure you a good night's sleep, we'll help you remember the date, FREE. Go to *www.wrapitupbooks.com*
and click on My Giving Guide.

3. Major Holidays

I don't know about you, but malls make me dizzy.
<u>Especially</u> the day after Thanksgiving.

Try going one, two or three days <u>before.</u>
>You won't believe how pleasant it is!
>Everything's ready before the rush.
>> • The merchandise is virtually untouched.
>> • Sales people are relaxed and have
>>   LOTS OF TIME to help YOU.
>> • There are virtually NO shoppers.
>>   (Why? You guessed it. They're either at the
>>   supermarket or already cooking.)

Bingo!
>Savor this delight with your best buddies.
>> • Give each of them a copy of *"Wrap It Up!"*
>>   ASAP as an early Holiday Gift
>> • Then closer to Christmas, schedule a mas-
>>   sage, lunch or a cocktail with the guys, so
>>   you can watch and gloat while the less in-
>>   formed males scowl and stress.

**Consider doing your Christmas shopping year
'round.**
>Shop right after Christmas for next year. Every-
>thing's reduced 50% or more.

Ho! Ho! Ho! Mrs. Claus will be so pleased! She'll know exactly how to fill the time you would ordinarily be shopping. I see opportunities here.

PSST: Santa usually poops out for anyone over 15 so get smart early. Help Santa with a few extras for the kid's, adult's and pet's stockings. And don't forget yourself.

"Where To Get
The #1 Best Idea
For Holiday Gifts!

Have your recipients write a letter to Santa. Pocket it vs. sending it to the North Pole.

Yup! This includes adults. Awww come-on. It's okay to play even if with a few gray hairs (showing or disguised). Don't miss the fun.

NO kids? Send a letter to Mr. or Mrs. Claus anyway. Stamp the envelope and address it to each other at home. You'll probably feel like an idiot. Do it anyway, laugh and have fun with it.

Be sure to add extra doses of laughter and joy to the Holidays.olidaysHolidays And remember that <u>everything does not need to be unwrapped in the first 30 minutes</u>.

Our family tradition was to allow unwrapping to take <u>days</u>. It was a delight. Our daughter got to play with and enjoy each new surprise, we got to play with new gadgets, and the holidays got relaxed.

4. Valentine's Day

EASY slam-dunk gifts that will make her smile.
TRAPS just waiting to ruin her day — and yours.

Slam-Dunk-Gifts	The Traps
Candy	Too cheap to chomp
Flowers	Wilted or almost
Card	You forgot it

Candy stores, florists and other retailers are
ready and waiting for you. So are the supermarkets and corner convenience stores. Most are pre-
pared for *emergency* purchases.

Trap avoidance:
>Plan ahead — BEFORE 4:45 on Valentine's Day.
>BEFORE the best stuff is picked over
>BEFORE the flowers are sold out
>BEFORE reservations are impossible

The Card:
>If they all sound too gooey, buy a blank card with
>a heart or flower design on the front and check
>out Chapter Eight, *50 Ways to Say "I Love You"*
>*Without saying it.*

Important Additives:

- Dinner for two is <u>not</u> a unique idea so make your reservations WAY AHEAD OF TIME. I suggest EARLY JANUARY.

- Get her a little dainty from the lingerie shop or department store

- Find a silver, gold, stone or ceramic heart on a chain to grace her pretty neck

- A hand-crafted, heart-shaped box with 3 chocolate truffles inside is tasty and provides a reusable treasure box when the edibles are gone

5. Mother's Day

Watch out! This is another jarring pothole if you're asleep at the wheel. Mother's Day demands careful planning and minimal cooking — if any — on your part.

The Gift:
Something personal from you – private delivery:
>Lingerie
>A spa basket of soap, bubble bath, lotion, a split
>>of champagne, two glasses, and some candles

The "instructions for use" are up to you. So is the presentation.

The Plan: Shhhh. This is a *"surprise"*
Breakfast in bed, gifts, cards.
>The Kids: Something made at school for Mom
>Everyone: A family crafted poster and/or
>>individual cards

If Granny is visiting, start the presentation parade with her, and have her join Mom in bed. Then serve breakfast in bed for the Two Moms. Take pictures.

PSST: If Granny is slightly bossy this tactic works particularly well.

The Menu: Everyone helps
(Except Mom and Granny)

Heated quiche	A tray
Cut up fruit or juice	Napkins & flatware
A rose for the tray	And a card

The Presentation:

Decorate yourself	Decorate the pets
Present the tray	Present gifts
Take pictures	

Ta-dah! You've done it! Good job. Well done.
Now bask in her delight and enjoy your own.
Guarantee you'll enjoy the rest of the day.
She'll see to that, and Granny can take the kids to
a movie.

The Day's young. Now what?
Restaurants are too loud and crowded.
<u>My vote is for a picnic.</u>
Buy a chicken-to-go. Fruit. Cookies. Drinks.
Napkins.
Go to your own back yard, the park, the beach,
take a hike and create your own picnic site.

PS: Be sure to pack a garbage bag and appoint a
clean-up committee ahead of time. Exclude Mom and
Granny — unless Granny insists.

6. Your Father's Day

Yeah! This is easy for you guys — us girls too, sort of.

Arrange a date with your Dad to:
- Get on the links
- On the court
- Board a boat (preferably on the water, but just looking at boats works, too)
- On a surfboard
- On the couch for chips, dip, beer, the game of the day or a family favorite DVD

One of my personal favorites was gathering several couples-with-kids, their Dads and Grand-Dads and go to a local park to play, sit, chat, bat, and eat fabulous food, and drink.

Everyone's happy. Especially you Dads.
Your Beloved will cheerfully put this together.

If your Dad's halfway across the country:
- Send cards (that's plural) <u>in advance</u>
- From the kids, too
- NO socks
- Call on THE day
- Send a book he would enjoy
- Find & send new guy-gadget
- Ship other "guy" stuff — early

7. Your Own "Special Day"

There's something particularly special about the dates
"Only You Two Share."
Flowers (Most of us NEVER tire of them)
- Have them delivered to the office or at
  home
- Deliver an armload of fresh cut flowers
  yourself
- Get them the night before, hide them, and
  put them on her dresser or in the bath-
  room (her side) before she gets up
- Get up and put them on her windshield
- Tuck cards in a kitchen drawer or in the
  frig

Music
- Remember "the music that went with your
  courtship"
- Be sure you find a way to play it through-
  out the day. On her iPOD.
- Into the phone when you call

Dinner
- Make reservations at your favorite place
- Sneak a card on the table when she's not
  looking

8. *The* Card For Every Occasion

Have At Least Two on hand for Every Event

- Always keep a supply handy for BIG and small occasions
- Plus a half dozen blank cards ready and waiting for your own inscription for a special event, or no event at all
- A personal expression of your affection

Check the Chapter Eight on 50 *Ways To Say, "I Love You", Without Saying It*

There are lots of places to get/buy cards
including:
Your Computer:
e-cards
Print-off cards
Supermarket
Car wash
Mega-Pharmacy
Minimarket
Florist
Card shop
Gift shop
Wine/Liquor store
Two-Minute Save Your Neck Solution:
A piece of plain white paper folded twice
Write "Happy ______________ on the front
Write your own personal message inside

9. The Kiss-And-Make-Up Gift
   8 Ways To Do Penance For A Flub

1. Acknowledge your screw-up and the recipient's
    feelings

2. Important you appear humble

3. Be honest, genuine and express your feelings

4. A <u>thoughtful act</u> on your part can ease her/his
    pain. Depending on the offense, the "act" can be
    anything from a sincere "I'm so sorry" plus a lov-
    ing hug, to a mink coat and diamond ring.

5. Forget the lame or blame excuses

6. Be vulnerable. Ask (beg) to be forgiven

7. Don't make any promises you can't/won't keep

8. VIP: AVOID making this a regular event!
    It's not good for your relationships, your health
    or your credit card.

PSST: If this is a recurring event be strong
and courageous and seek professional help . . .
everyone will love you for it.

The only currency in this bankrupt
world is what you share with
someone else when you're un-cool.

Philip Seymour Hoffman

In Almost Famous

52 WHAT-TO-GIVE GIFT IDEAS

16 Quick Gift Solutions

1. Jewelry
2. Accessories
3. Colognes/Fragrances
4. Bath and Body Delights
5. Books
6. Art
7. Theater/Concerts/Movie Tickets
8. Cameras & Accessories
9. High Tech Gadgets
10. Spa Treatments
11. Hobby/Craft Supplies
12. Home/Office Decor Items
13. Musical Instruments
14. Sports Wear
15. Sports Gear
16. Your Own Special Creation

36 More Gift Ideas
The Original Quick Gift Solutions

1. JEWELRY

   General Styles:

- Fine Jewelry
- Costume Jewelry
- Trendy, dramatic, bulky, geometric
- Traditional
- Ethnic
- Eclectic
- Semiprecious stones
- Colorful glass or crystal
- Art jewelry
- Solid gold
- Sterling silver
- Precious stones

   Finger Rings

- Borrow one from her jewelry box.
- Take it to any jeweler. Have it sized.
- Write down the size in *Wrap It Up!* and/or your *Pocket Informant©*
- Put the ring back before it's missed

   Earrings
   Toe Rings
   Necklaces
   Wrist and Ankle Bracelets

2. ACCESSORIES
   Handbags
   Hats
   Belts
   Shoes
   Shawls/Shoulder Wraps
   Scarves/Neck, Hip, Both
   Costume/Exotic Jewelry

3. COLOGNES/FRAGRANCES
   Colognes are lighter than perfume
   Fragrance can be:
        Heavily Scented
        Light Fragrance
        Floral
        Herbal

4. BATH AND BODY DELIGHTS
   Oil, sea salt, bubbles, herbs, rose petals
   Bath Fragrances — lots of choices
   Skin brushes, bath sponges, pumice stone for
      heels & elbows
   Body lotion
   Body tanning lotion
   Softening foot crèmes
   Shaving crèmes
   Bath slippers
   Terry cloth robe
   Sexy robe to go with a glass of champagne

5. BOOKS
    Mysteries
    Romance
    Career/Self-Development
    Spiritual
    Motivational
    Non-Fiction
    Business
    Biographies
    Craft
    Cooking
    Travel

6. ART
    Visit a museum or galleries together — Observe
    what she likes:
        Contemporary, Modern,
        Impressionist, Landscape
        Figurative (has people in it)
        Abstract (just shapes, colors, form)
        Portraits
        Old oils (landscapes, portraits, animals)
        Watercolors
        Work on paper
        Posters
        Prints

7. THEATER/CONCERT/MUSICAL/
    MOVIE TICKETS
    Jazz
    Classical
    Country
    Rock/Rap/Hip-Hop
    Full concert orchestra
    Choral
    Music of the 50's / 60's / 70's +

8. CAMERAS
    Digital
    35 mm
    For the pro/am
        Lenses
        Umbrellas
        Special carrying cases
        Lighting apparatus
        Stands

9. HIGH TECH ACCESSORIES
    The new gadget of the day
    New software
    Newest cell phone
    Computer/TV accessories, games

10. SPA TREATMENTS
    Day of Beauty at a Spa
    Full Body Massage
    Facial

11. HOBBY / CRAFT SUPPLIES
     Needlepoint, quilting, knitting, crochet
     Weaving supplies, yarn or a weaving matching
     Painting supplies
     Unpainted furniture, art objects
     Flower arranging classes and/or supplies
The list can be long — just observe, listen to requests
and put vital information in your *Pocket Informant©*

12. DECORATOR ITEMS — For home or office
     Vases are always appreciated — especially if <u>you</u>
         occasionally fill them with flowers
         (PSST: That's a hint.)
     Decorative crystal or glass art items
     Accent pillows for the bedroom, sofa or favorite
         chair
     Picture frame for the desk

13. MUSICAL INSTRUMENTS
     If they have one — Consider lessons to hone
         skills, sheet music, recording equipment
     A musical instrument they have always wanted
         and lessons

14. SPORTSWEAR — HEAD TO TOE
     Hats
     Clothing
     All-weather gear from rafting wet suits to snow
         parkas
     Sports specific shoes

15. SPORTS GEAR
     Skis
     Golf clubs
     Tennis racket
     Fly fishing pole
     Kayak
     Surfboards
     Skateboards
     In-line skates
     Badminton racket
     Paddle tennis racket
     Ping-pong paddle
     You know the drill

16. YOUR OWN SPECIAL CREATIONS
For you men with a little or a lot of creativity in your
DNA, just know your Recipients will go wild over
anything you create or make just for them such as:
     Your own poetry
     Hand-crafted wood carvings
     A painting or sketches
     A paper weight out of rocks you collected
        together
     An original song you wrote for your Heart Throb
     A CD you recorded of your Beloved's favorite
        music
     A romantic dinner or breakfast you make

____

____

____

About 4″ Heels

HEY. If you've never seen your Dream Girl in 4″ heels, <u>make inquiries before buying</u>.

Say, "What do you think about hose 4″ heels?"
If she says, "You gotta be kidding???!!!"
<u>It can mean one of two things</u>:

1. She wears them a lot and you haven't noticed — Idiot!

Or

2. She can't wear them at all.
Hope for the latter and clarify anyway!
After this, be more observant.

VIP: Some of the newest WOW-looking shoes are priced from \$295–\$750+. (That's no joke.) Make sure your woman and wallet are ready for such an extravagance. You can get a great looking pair for under \$125. Check out department stores and mid-priced shoe specialty shops. Set your <u>price \$\$\$ limits</u> as part of your criteria.

What about <u>Underwear???!!! You ask?</u>
Please gentlemen, tell me you NEVER use the word
<u>underwear</u>. Sounds so baggy.
So un-romantic. So Gramma.

PSST: <u>Omit the word "underwear" totally</u> unless you're in the boy's or men's department
and buying for yourself, your dad or your son.

Got Sexy Lingerie Purchase Jitters?
If intimate apparel is a difficult purchase for you, just
go to a good department store and say, "I need help"
to the first sales person (preferably female) who
smiles at you. She'll take care of the rest. And the
store will take it back if you goof.

A Helpful Lingerie Size Alert
Scant, sexy lingerie sizing is tricky. If she's a teenie,
tiny person size Petite to Small is pretty reliable. If
she's still slender, with narrow hips and thin legs Size
Small may still work. Though she may wear a size 6
in pants and skirts, if she has even a hint of curves go
for the Medium Size. Its still little. For a size 10 or 12
figure, Large is best. If she's edging to size 14 or more,
best be clear on that with the salesperson.

VIP: There's nothing worse or more uncom-
fortable than scant lingerie that squeezes,
pinches or crawls up where it doesn't belong.

REMEMBER . . .
Diamonds are a girl's best friend.
So is anything that comes in a small blue box tied
with white ribbon or a King Size Bow®

PSST: I know. Recipients are impossible.
Sorry about that. Just remember these treats
are good for your reputation. Just accept it
and enjoy the rewards they're so eager to give.

For "where-to-find-it" suggestions check Chapter
Eight and *www.wrapitupbooks.com*

FOOTBALL TIPS TO MASTER GIFT-BUYING HAND-OFFS

Okay, you're gonna like this gift-buying hand-off for recipients like your mother, aunt, sister, secretary, etc. Pass the gift-buying task on to someone who knows the recipient. Your wife/lifemate.
This gift-purchase strategy is a slam-dunk, touchdown, hole-in-one — IF you handle the ball right.

Here's How To Structure *The* Hand-Off

1. First, wipe that smirk off your face.
2. Hit the TV MUTE. I know it's hard, but it's worth it. You don't want to sabotage the play.
3. Use the *Sandwich Play©* to successfully hand off the gift buying to someone else and get back to the game—slowly. Sit back! Relax! Enjoy!

PSST: Before you launch the *Sandwich Play©* — keep in mind that failure here can "put your tight end in a sling," so proceed thoughtfully.

Mark this page, Coach. You can use The *Sandwich Play©* in lots of situations — at work, at home or play.

Here's How The *Sandwich Play©* Works.
Think of a roast beef sandwich on rye.

The Top Slice of Rye Bread:
Start off with your winning style,
> "Honey, you are so intuitive about what people
> want and like, I wonder if you could help me
> out?"

Think they're on to your sudden sweet-talk, right?
Probably, but don't count on it.
We're all fools for sweet-talk – even if it's repetitive
and oh-so-obvious. Too much of <u>this</u> good thing is
<u>really good</u>.

Next, the Beef:
Try something like this,
> "I'd really appreciate it if you could you pick out
> a gift and card for your mother or Great Auntie
> Mame's birthday."

If such a request for help is *old* news, and your Number One is up to your tricks, and the answer's a blank stare, a little humor can turn the tables.

"Such as?" you ask. Reasonable question.
Turn on that big irresistible grin of yours — the one
they like — get down on your knees and beg!

One of two things will happen.
> You'll both laugh and they'll say "Okay, okay.
> You win — again."

> Or you may already have some thoughts —
> clever man that you are — on how another sport-
> ing performance (other than TV) might score
> points in your favor.

The Bottom Slice of the *Sandwich Play*:
It's the punch line. The clincher. So wrap it up along
these lines.
> "I know you're busy, so please buy something for
> yourself as my *thank you*."
Smile lovingly and DON'T rush back to the TV or
your favorite hobby.

If you're new at this and think she'll buy a Mercedes
or a fine leather jacket while she's out, forget it.
That only works once and we girls know it.

PSST: If you have one of those rare Love-
Objects you really <u>can't</u> trust with your credit
card at any time, slip them some cold cash
and hope your Mother or Auntie Mame gets
the lion's share.

If all attempts fail:
Curl up during the commercials with the latest issue
of a good mail order catalog — NOT hunting gear or
home improvement equipment and
    Pick and pay
    Grab another snack
    Get back to your afternoon indulgence

Any Way You Cut It — You Win!

By the way, the *Sandwich Play* is an invaluable tactic to apply in other situations such as touchy conversations with adults or teens, delivering bad news, or as a more productive response to tiresome complaining.

Might want to tattoo the *Play Strategy* on your arm if your memory's short — or keep it handy in your *Pocket Informant©*.

I guarantee it will dramatically:
- Improve all your communications
- Enhance relationships
- Reduce conflicts
- Help avoid unhappy feelings in all directions
- Be a role model for your kids and adult observers
- Replace make-up gifts with smiles, handshakes and hugs

It seems rather incongruous
that in a society of
super sophisticated communication,
we often suffer from
a shortage of listeners.

Erma Brombeck

The 5 MAGICAL GIFTS

1. Say "I Love You" Every Day

2. Really Listen

3. Be Fully Engaged In The Moment

4. Offer Your Smile Frequently

5. Bestow A Gentle Touch Often

5 MAGICAL GIFTS
E-X-P-A-N-D-E-D

1. SAY "I LOVE YOU" EVERY DAY

> "No thanks. I think it sounds forced after a
> while."
> Ever ask the Object-Of-Your-Affection about
> that? No?
> You might be surprised.

Granted *it* may not *always* sound as though you're
having a fit of passion, yet, most like to hear it anyway. If you get tired of "repeating yourself" check
Chapter 8 for some new ways to say *it*.

2. REALLY LISTEN

<u>Asking questions</u> is a key to unlocking the mystery.
And to understand us, you need to master the "Art Of
Asking Questions."
We never make it easy, do we? But you'll appreciate
the results.

See Outta Sight Insights© at the end of this chapter to
discover more about how to invite conversation and
intimacy's through questions.

Women don't mean what they say,
and don't say what they mean.
You have to figure that out
by what's in between.

Carolyn Johnson

A Beautiful Southern Belle

ABOUT LISTENING BETWEEN THE LINES AND ASKING QUESTIONS TO CLARIFY UNDERSTANDING.

Listening *behind/inside* the *speaking* is imperative if you want to understand and be understood.

Works in personal, professional and playtime situations. Don't get it? Hang on for two minutes.

The process is simple and it works with anybody. Male or female. Any age. Even teens.

Try this and practice:

THEY SAY: What do you think about the idea of ____________________________?

YOU: I'm not sure I get what you mean. Can you tell me more about ______________ so I'm clear?

THEY SAY: (Hopefully) Sure. And then a re-casting of what they said.

YOU: Sorry. Still don't get it.

THEY SAY: Okay. Let me say it this way. . . .

YOU: So, you 're saying that . . . _______________
_________ (repeat her statement as you understand
it.) Is that right?

THEY SAY: "Exactly."

You did it! And guess what? You'll have the information you need to respond, and they'll be impressed
that ". . . you were actually listening and responding
. . . thoughtfully." What could be better?

If they're of the feminine gender, their friends will
hear about it and applaud your qualities and ask for
the conversation recipe. Hand her a couple of copies
of *"Wrap It Up!"* for her friends.

You both learned important things about each other
that will be of value to your relationship whether it's
as friends, lovers, co-workers, boss or beast across the
hall.

Generally, this asking questions is good for your reputation and your ego — and your counterpart will be
moved to find ways to express her appreciation —
over and over again.

Three good things will now happen.

1. You'll get a clear answer and will understand it.

2. They'll be awed because you listened and asked questions.

3. You'll get <u>major points — maybe more.</u>

PSST: Keep going fellas. You're on a roll.

This kind of first-class listening can deliver a lifetime of good things!
Guaranteed.
And you'll keep your hair longer.

The greatest gift you can
give anyone is your
complete and undivided attention.
If you think that's a *simple* gift,
you haven't tried giving it.

Cleo Brynmar

3. BE FULLY ENGAGED IN THE MOMENT

To a Recipient that means:

- Put the TV on mute or turn it off when a conversation begins. Tough I know.

PSST: Turning it OFF is a brave and best choice

- Ask if the conversation can wait until half-time so you can really pay attention

- NOT planning what you'll say next while someone's speaking

- NOT asleep during their favorite/familiar monologue

- NOT waiting to deliver — heaven help <u>them</u> — another of your monologues

- NEVER ignoring what's been said so you can get back to <u>your</u> last remark or Monday night football

4. OFFER YOUR SMILE

- Use it often

- Use it when it's not expected. *Never* as a sneer

- Use it in addition to, or instead of, words when it means something kind not a, "yeah, right. . . ."

- Use it in a traffic jam. With a friendly wave instead of a *gesture*

- Know when NOT to use it

5. BESTOW A GENTLE TOUCH

A touch delivers a special message all its own from the giver to the receiver. There is a wide range of ways you can reach out and touch someone.
- In business and social situations we use a handshake, a pat on the back, a friendly hug, a genuine — not sarcastic — air kiss

- In personal situations it can be holding hands, a caring caress

- Holding a crying child, a troubled adult, or a grieving friend

- Offering a hand to a stranger, a person struggling to cross a busy street, a lost child

They Are All True Gifts

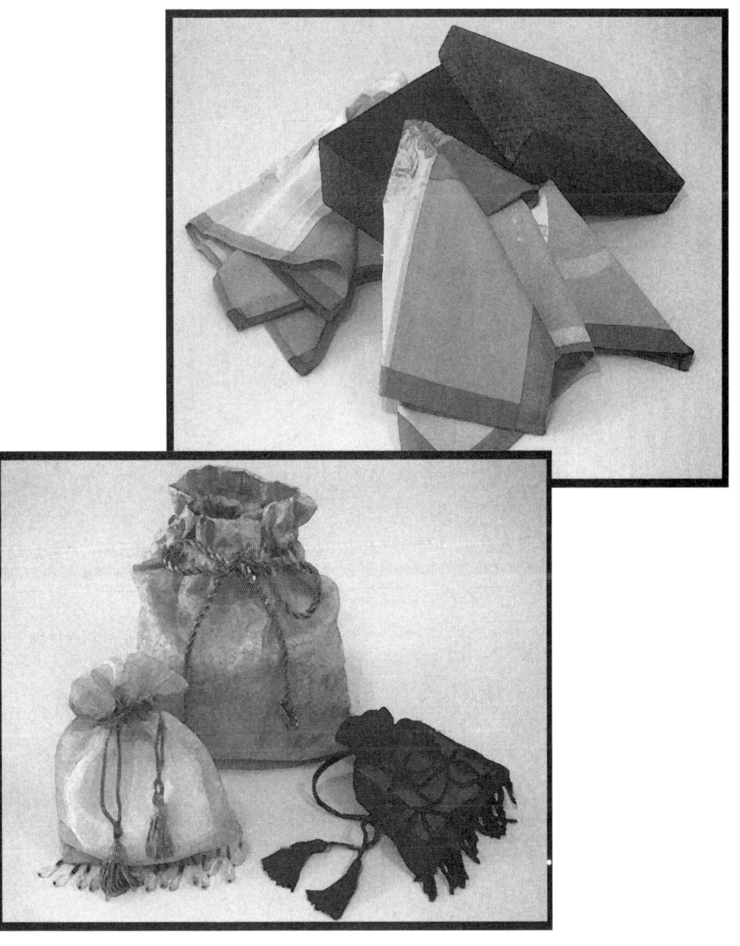

We've all heard it time and again;
in battle, in business, and in life,

*"You never get a second chance
to make a first impression!"*

The moment of a Gift's
first sighting — it's like fireworks!
An explosion of color drama forming
glittering shapes that fill the sky.
We Oooooh. We ahhhhh.
And we never forget the first
awesome impression.

It's the <u>same</u> when you
present yourself or your gift.
Like fireworks, the combination makes
an unforgettable first impression and
creates excitement and anticipation.
And we Recipients never forget.

That's WOW-inspiring wrapping.
And <u>anyone</u> can do it.

WOW-INSPIRING WRAPPING

&

PERSUASIVE PRESENTATIONS

There Are Only TWO Wrapping Options:

1. Someone does it for you

2. You do it yourself

They both work.

You choose.

SOMEONE ELSE DOES IT

AT THE STORE

1. Ask for the store's basic FREE wrap.
    Don't panic if it's just a simple paper bag with handles plus tissue and a small bow.
    Ask for LOTS of tissue and TWO bows, and you've got WOW.

2. Pay for a fancy wrap.
    It's worth its weight in WOW.

    "My preference" you ask? I like Number 1.
    Oodles of colored tissue that sticks out of a colorful bag and some sort of a big bow.
    The store can do it. You can do it, too. Read on.

ASK YOUR TALENTED NEIGHBOR

This works best if the neighbor is someone who loves to wrap.

You may want to proffer a bottle of wine if there are several to be wrapped and you want the opportunity to call on those talents again.

DO IT YOURSELF WRAPPING
Simple Recipes For Success

7 THINGS TO REMEMBER!

1. Check your *Pocket Informant©* or *www.wrapitupbooks.com* for the "Wrapping Ingredients" you need for any occasion.

2. Keep your *Pocket Informant©* in your wallet for last minute. I-forgot fill-ins.

3. Grab a beer and your *"Wrap It Up!"* then wrap it up.

4. Munch a breath mint

5. Prepare your adorable smile

6. Present the gift

7. Enjoy the rewards!

The Guys Wrapping Survival Kit©

1. Colorful paper bags in different sizes and colors,
    with handles

2. A couple rolls of basic, patterned or solid colored
    wrapping paper

3. Lots of tissue. Excesses of white for filler.
    Plenty of assorted, seasonal, accent colors.
    Yellow   Pink   Light Green
    Dark Blue   Purple   Baby Blue
    Red   Green   Gold/Silver

4. Assorted pre-made, stick-on bows

5. A couple rolls of ribbon and fat yarn

6. Clear tape

7. Scissors

8. A selection of cards, from special occasions to
    decorative blanks

9. For the Wrapping Chef, tie on anything.
    Fake flowers   Decorative hearts
    Small stuffed animals   Kids play jewelry
    A toy bunny or car   Small party-favors
    A backyard leafy twig   A garden flower

Wait! Hold It! Stop!
Don't Toss Out The Sunday Paper!!!
Until You Set Aside The *Creative Wrapping Paper* — AKA The . . .

Sunday Comic Section
Book Review Section
Entertainment Section
Travel Section
The Sports Section
Any Full Page Ads that match a special interest
such as:
Jewelry
Clothing
Financial
Business
Decorating

How To Use ~~Throw-Away~~ Creative Paper For Wrapping

These "throw-away sheets of newspaper" can be transformed into creative, delightful, even thoughtful, gift-wrappings. Wrap and see.

For Sportswear and Sports Gear
Use the Sports Section. Just make sure a cute muscle man is visible. Makes the package look so much more enticing.

For Clothing And Intimate Apparel.
You'll find plenty of suitable advertising pages in the main news section.
- Intimate apparel. AKA lingerie, bras and panties, sleepwear and, heaven forbid, underwear? Does anyone say "underwear"? Please say "No!!!"

For Books.
You guessed it. The Sunday Book Section.

For Tickets To a Live Performance or Dinner at The Newest Hot Spot.
The Entertainment Section.

For Flowers.

From the supermarket or guy at the freeway exit.
Add a bow, you're good to go.
(Do we care from where? No! It's the flowers that
count!! As long as they're not wilted or brown
around the edges.)

They're usually pre-bundled into a small bouquet
snuggled in a clear cellophane wrapper.
Just pay your money. Go home happy.

High Tech Stuff.
A New Cell Phone. Computer. New Software.

If it's an Apple®, iMAC® or an iPod® stick with
Apple's delicious bags.
They have almost the same impact as the famous
Tiffany-Blue Box-with-White-Ribbon.
They both create recipient-putty in your hands.

Otherwise check out the newspaper business, financial or main news sections for the perfect
sheet of wrapping paper. Add a bow or string,
your adorable smile and present it with a million-
dollar flourish.

The VIP Wrapper Option.

To enhance your own creativity or enjoyment of
the wrapping experience add a beer, glass of
wine or soft drink to the "wrapping ingredients list." DON'T WORRY. BE HAPPY.

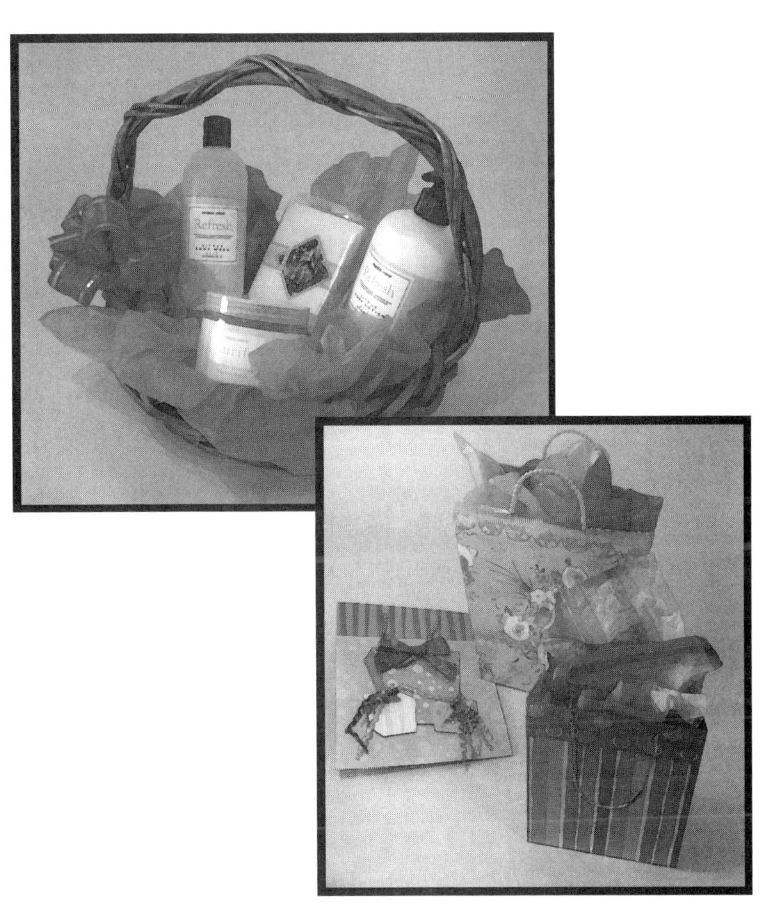

Outta Sight Insights©
Wrapping for all levels of rappers.

CREATE YOUR OWN ORIGINAL —
MESSY WORKS !

PSST: Hard to believe but yesterday's paper or grocery bag, tied with dirty old string from the garage gives us genuine joy and delight. Really. Could be a favorite. Okay. Well, not for every gift forever. But it's a good fallback position. Once anyway.

TIPS FOR THE GIFT &
WRAPPING CHALLENGED

Okay. So, you got the I—*almost*—forgot gift by the last whisker on your chinny-chin-chin. Good for you. Only you and I have to know it was a close call.

The bare bones drug store shooed you out and closed — they didn't have ANY wrapping stuff anyway.

In case you don't already know, a naked gift just won't cut it. Blows your last-minute cover.

Covering (wrapping) your gift is the <u>only</u> option. Consider the supermarket. They usually have basics like white tissue and pre-made bows. You could also climb out of the box and get creative yourself.

If the gift is bath and body delights, you can always wrap them in a towel or pillowcase. Sounds nuts, doesn't it? Not so. Carefully pulled together it can be a dramatic presentation. Would be good idea if the towel or pillowcase were new or at least clean.

Properly presented, the last-minute nature of this precious offering may go unnoticed. Whew!

Here's where repetition <u>doesn't</u> get repetitious.

Seeing her face light up when you hand her the package, especially when it's <u>not expected</u> is the gift back to you. Feels good doesn't it!

And the chances of becoming the beneficiary of a particularly nice dinner for two has just increased tenfold.

Keep the trend going. You'll both love it.

CREATIVE WRAPPING
FOR THE BEGINNER

In the beginning men's hands were designed for hunting, surviving battle, wielding a chainsaw, swinging a baseball bat, roping a bull on the run and other such strength-demanding, manly endeavors. They still are.

You noticed gift-wrapping is not on the list. That's okay. It's not expected.

It should be no surprise to you that we girls flee when it's time for you to wrestle with wrapping.
Not because it's funny — we know it's a guy thing.
But because it's painful. For you, I imagine.

Starting now the pain is gone.

You'll find some fool-proof-basics just ahead as well as some easy creative, inventive and original wrapping suggestions guaranteed to elicit a smile and, at the very least, a nice hug from your Radiant Recipient.

Just remember to vary wrapping styles throughout the year so they're not totally predictable.

Always <u>present yourself well</u> with style or flair. If you're just arriving home from work, take time to freshen up, squirt on some cologne, put on a fresh shirt, a clean smile and you're set for a special time. We appreciate those things a lot.

WRAPPING FOR THE EXPERIENCED

To you artist types, creative types, manual dexterity types, what can I say that you don't already know or haven't improved upon to the nth degree?
"Keep doing what you're doing."

I applaud you, as well as whomever it was that taught you this important art of giving. Please thank your teacher and spread your wisdom and this book among your buddies.

Even the most expert-at-giving of you wonderful men aren't always equally skilled wrappers.

You Pros may want to scan Beginner Strategies for some new ideas.

EXPERIENTIAL PRESENTATIONS

Tuck a ring or bauble inside "her" birthday cake.
  The bakery (or chef) will happily cooperate.
  If it's a do-it-yourself . . .
  - Poke a small hole in the cake.
  - Tuck in the ring.
  - Dampen a knife and carefully move icing over the "spot"

You can put a package inside a gingerbread house.

If you're dining out, arrange ahead of time to present the gift as "The special appetizer or dessert you've ordered."

Have the restaurant put the gift under a rounded lid they lift off to reveal the entrée.
Shazam! This time it's her gift.

You've got it made, Guy. She'll love it and doubtless figure out some nice ways to say "Thank you."

If it's organic body wash and cream, maybe in a subtle fragrance, wrap it in something appropriate to the gift and sniff later.
>A pretty towel
>An elegant pillowcase
>(New is best. Used okay. But please tell me it's not necessary to say, "Clean is imperative.")
>A wicker basket loaded with tissue
>A pretty box that's perfect for your love notes to her and keepsakes later on.

Yes! Tie them with pretty ribbon or a big pre-made bow available at any card store, mega pharmacy and variety store combo or well-stocked supermarket.

Most lingerie specialty stores have great wrapping available.
Just ask. And always ask for EXTRA tissue.
(One sheet looks so thin.)

WHAT TO DO WITH THE
ONCE-IN-A-LIFETIME GIFT

It's a CAR?
Ohmygawd. Are you serious?
You're serious! This is way cool. Great idea.
You're not kidding, right?

Okay. Here's one way to present it:
    First park it at some perfect "viewing place."
    NOT your garage or carport.
    We want a little titillating suspense here.
    Try a nearby park or greenbelt.
    Remember the King Sized Bow on the hood
    Put the naked key in an unmarked box.
    The duller the better. Even a used box.
    DON'T tie anything around it.

"How tacky" will be the visceral reaction. (This is so
fun.) Ignore the initial hostility, and gently guide your
Love Bud to the "Presentation Point."

They'll likely, "Squeal!!!" And say, "Thank you! Thank
you. Anything you want honey."

PSST: That's one of your rewards. For at least
24 hours. Maybe longer. "I'm all yours my
love," is your only answer.

I suggest YOU design your evening from this point
forward — including a sitter if you have kids.

King Size Bows

Here's another way to take her by surprise.

Take notes or mark this page.
This is NOT as complicated as it sounds, and I guarantee will garner unimaginable rewards.

Plan the evening. Dinner at her favorite restaurant. Flowers already on the table. Baby sitter scheduled.

Pick up THE new car and arrange with a buddy to meet you at the restaurant. The one where you're having a dinner-for-two tonight.
Park THE car somewhere prominent.
Make a deal with the valet.
Give him THE key.
Have your buddy drive you back to <u>your</u> car and drive home.

Freshen up for dinner and escort your Lovely to <u>your car as usual</u> and drive to the restaurant. She won't suspect a thing.Present a loving card over dinner.

After dinner, have the valet get THE car. The Valet opens the <u>driver's</u> door and signals your Succulent One to "get in . . ."
             "This isn't our car," she'll say!
YOU have only <u>one</u> reply here,
       "I know. It's yours! Happy ___________."

The rest of the evening is up to you. Have fun.

There are only two ways
of spreading love;
To be the giver or
The recipient who passes it forward.

Ann Hult Crowell

Chapter Seven

WHERE TO GET IT

<u>High Quality Specialty:</u>
>L. L. Bean
>Coach
>MAC
>Gucci
>Cache
>Fendi
>Origins
>Dior
>Louis Vuitton
>Dooney & Bourke

<u>Other Quality Specialty:</u>
>Godiva Chocolatier
>Sees Candy
>Crate & Barrel
>Pottery Barn
>Sharper Image
>Restoration Hardware

<u>Clothing Stores:</u>
    Nordstrom
    Apropos
    St. John
    Ann Taylor
    Giorgio Armani
    Saks Fifth Avenue
    Ralph Lauren
    DKNY
    Bebe
    Chico's
    Neiman Marcus
    Max Mara

<u>Other Top-Rated Clothing Stores:</u>
    Amazon.com Clothing
    Eddie Bauer
    Orvis
    L. L. Bean
    J. Crew
    Gap
    Coldwater Creek
    Macy's
    Land's End
    Old Navy
    Spiegel
    Woolrich
    Bluefly's
    Big Dog Sportswear
    Ashford

Wal Mart
Target
Sears
JC Penney
Mervyns
Kohl's

Fine Jewelry Stores:
    Mardo Jewelry Inc.
    Mikimoto
    Cartier
    Swarovski
    Tiffany

Artistic/Costume Jewelry Stores:
    Chico's
    Department Stores
    Local Specialty Shops
    On Consignment Shops
    Antique Shops

Colognes/Fragrance/Bath/Beauty Items:
    Nordstrom
    Bloomingdales
    Macy's
    Dillards
    Expanded Pharmacys such as:
        Walgreen's
        Sav-On/CVC

<u>Hobbies:</u>
   Scrapbooking/Hobby Shop
   Knitting/Crocheting
   Sewing
   Quilting
   Photography
   China Painting

<u>Miscellaneous:</u>
   Theater Tickets
   Concert Tickets
   Ballet Tickets
   Museums/Art Galleries
   Dinner
   Books/CDs
   Weekend Get-Away
   Spas/Treatments
   Florists
   Sports Equipment — Ski, biking, hiking, etc.
   Luggage
   Surprise Overnight — You arrange the sitter

<u>Women's Plus Size Clothing:</u>
   Nordstrom
   Avenue (14–32)
   Catherine's (16W–34W)
   Eddie Bauer Plus Sizes
   Elisabeth by Liz Claiborne
   Fashion Bug
   JC Penney

Jessica London
Junonia (14 and up)
Just My Size (up to 4X and 32W)
J. Jill Plus Sizes (14W–28W)
Kohl's Plus Sizes
La Redoute (up to size 26)
Land's End (18W–26W)
Lane Bryant (14W–44W)
Liz Claiborne Woman (14–24)
Making It Big
Silhouettes (12W–34W)
Size Appeal
Soft Surroundings (18–24)
Torrid (Young women 15-29/sizes 12–26)
Ulla Popken (12–34)
Alight.com (14W–28W)
Igigi (12–32)
Kiyonna (14 up)
Sydney's Closet (14–44)
TravelSmith Plus Sizes
Womensuits.com

<u>Intimate Apparel, Lingerie:</u>
Victoria's Secret
Bare Necessities
Chadwick's of Boston
Essential Apparel
Frederick's of Hollywood
Inner-Self
Undergear.com

<u>Shoes/Footwear:</u>
    Nordstrom
    Bali
    Gucci
    Stuart Weitzman
    Happy Feet
    Johnston & Murphy
    Payless Shoe Source
    Shoes Avenue
    Vans

<u>Maternity Clothing:</u>
    Motherhood Maternity
    A Pea In The Pod
    Maternity Mall
    Mimi Maternity
    Motherhood Nursing
    Motherwear
    Maternity at Babystyle

<u>Stores For Children:</u>
    Yellow Pages is a great starting point:
    Major Department Stores
    Toy Stores
    Children's Clothing Stores
    Children's Shoe Stores

If I love myself I love you.
If I love you I love myself.

Rumi

50 WAYS TO SAY "I LOVE YOU"

(Even Without Saying It)

50 Ways To Say, Write, Express Your Feelings

1. You hear my thoughts and answer them without speaking.

2. You listen with your heart and know mine.

3. Every new discovery about you reminds me it's no accident we are together.

4. The mere sound of your voice awakens my soul and makes my heart sing.

5. You make my heart sing with music I never knew was there.

6. You make me feel larger than life.

7. Arrange a surprise birthday party for your Honeysuckle.

8. I could conquer anything aided only by the love I have for you.

9. Make a rose petal path from the front door to a surprise you have waiting.

10. Your smile lights every corner of my being.

11. Write a poem of your own around something you love about your Dear One.

12. I woke up in the darkest part of night bathed in warm sunshine and realized it was simply being in your presence.

13. Arrange a massage at home for her.

14. I want to dust off your wings so you can soar as never before and realize all your dreams.

15. Plan a hot air balloon ride to romantic heights.

16. I want to reflect back to you the light and love you radiate on me every day.

17. Postpone the chores and be lazy one Saturday a month.

18. Your beauty stops my heart.

19. Put your favorite picture of her on a "T" shirt.

20. Get her favorite picture of you for hers.

21. You take my breath away and return it in ways that move into my heart and make it larger.

22. Bring home a heart-shaped cookie when it's not Valentine's Day.

23. My heart wants to love you even more, yet I can't imagine how that could be possible.

24. Next time you're out for dinner whisper "You're magnificent" in her ear.

25. You have captured me entirely.

26. Walk outside after dark and look for the Milky Way

27. I have never felt so whole.

28. When I'm away from you're tucked in my heart.

29. Hide notes in the pockets of their *off season clothes to be found later.*

30. Tell me another way I can shower you with love and joy.

31. I love your hair when it's wind-blown and your cheeks are flushed.

32. I hope your heart hears mine even when we're asleep.

33. My world came alive the moment I met you.

34. Check the weather calendar and watch a full moonset — wrapped in the same blanket.

35. I want to protect and keep your heart and soul safe forever.

36. I respect and cherish you and always will.

37. Write a love note on your skin and make them find it.

38. It's raining today but sunny in your presence. Thank you for being my sunshine.

39. Buy an incredibly soft blanket *today* to wrap her up on the first cold night.

40. There isn't anything I can't do in the presence of your smile.

41. Get a special frame for your favorite picture of Loved One smiling your favorite smile.

42. Buy the groceries and cook twice a month. Vary the nights. <u>Occasional</u> take-out is OK.

43. Your love has made me sure of myself.

44. Rent a romantic movie to watch in bed.

45. "Not having tasted a single cup of your wine I'm
    already drunk." Rumi

46. Put an exquisite bottle of wine, a small plate of
    cheese, bread squares, two glasses and napkins on
    a tray and escort your Sweetheart to the bedroom.

47. Call during work and say, "When I think about
    you in the middle of my day ________.

48. Listen to your Darling's fantasies and make them
    a reality.

49. Make reservations at a nearby Bed and Breakfast
    and play tourist.

50. My fondest memory of you is . . .

Get Caught Being Yourself.

This is where small acts of giving
become the foundation,
the bonding solution, the buttress of a
loving relationship
built to last.

Ann Hult Crowell

76 PRICELESS GIFTS ... AND MOST DON'T COST A PENNY

1. Say "I love you" every day

2. Plan a "Mystery Date" for sometime next month

3. Bake homemade muffins together

4. Roll up the rug and dance together at home

5. Weed the garden without being asked

6. Arrive with flowers for no reason

7. Say that you're enchanted / captivated / enam
   ored

8. "I really appreciate the way you _______________"

9. Be patient

10. Celebrate their birthday every day for a month

11.   A hot bath and a cool drink is a warm thank you

12.   Mail a little box of candy conversation hearts

13.   Be interested and supportive of their career

14.   Always kiss each other upon departing

15.   Be there for each other — always

16.   Write "I love you" in new fallen snow

17.   Help create an environment of love. Start now

18.   When she's had an especially tense week, surprise her with dinner out and one-night hotel stay

19.   Fight fair

20.   Give of your time

21.   Handle with care

22.   Inspire your partner with your expressions of love

23.   Use gummy letter shaped candies to spell out love messages

24.   Bring her the first cup of AM coffee

25. Send a bouquet made of little love notes fashioned into flowers

26. Keep your memories alive

27. Listen to each other

28. Give her a theme gift: one pink rose, pink lingerie, a pink candle and bottle of pink champagne

29. Never go to bed angry

30. Hand write and mail a sexy message (put "Confidential" on the envelope to keep it private)

31. Offer to handle an unpleasant chore

32. Praise your partner

33. Hide a ring in a rose bud — wait for it to bloom

34. Give of your quality time

35. Respect their feelings

36. Say what you feel

37. Understand your differences

38. Wash their car

39. Zero in on little passions

40. Visit a butterfly aviary

41. Give her a scarf that illustrates her hobby

42. Hide favorite candy in the dresser or desk drawer

43. Spoil your Special One every day for a week

44. Repeat the week now and then

45. Leave a love message in her lingerie drawer

46. Take a moonlight stroll

47. Enjoy a sunrise picnic

48. Take the day off for your Valentine

49. Give your modern gal a piece of antique jewelry

50. Create a "Romantic Idea Jar"

51. Send her a bouquet of balloons for no special reason

52. Sing a romantic song on her answering machine

53. Towel her dry after she showers

54. Tuck a sexy message in her purse

55. Go out on an extravagant date

56. When dining out, sit next to each other

57. Kiss under water

58. Watch romantic movies together

59. Hide a note in a jacket/coat pocket

60. Be the "Chippendale Fantasy Dancer"

61. Give a gift based on Beloved's favorite TV show

62. Triple your time spent on foreplay — she'll adore you for it

63. Do something for her you hate to do

64. Return to the place where you first met

65. Put earrings in a glass of champagne

66. Add to her collection of porcelain angels

67. Wrap gifts in bright red

68. Celebrate Valentine's Day, every day for a week

69. Feed her grapes on a lazy Saturday

70. Before getting out of bed, say, "I'm so thankful I have you in my life . . ."

71. Turn off the TV and just be together

72. Be genuinely interested in what she's saying

73. Plan sensual surprises

74. Compliment her on what she's wearing

75. Make homemade ice cream together

76. Eat it in bed and watch a romantic movie

Outta Sight Insights©
Abundant Treasures Await You

ABOUT THOSE PRICELESS GIFTS THAT DON'T COST A PENNY

In my research, we Objects-Of-Your-Affection willingly admit we're unpredictable, quixotic, and mysterious. Irritating at times. Frustrating. Impossible to figure out. And irresistible. It's a girl thing.

Happily this gift category is painless. It costs no money. Just a little time and thought. And your Recipients know *that time and thought alone are priceless commodities.*

Some Loved Ones might need help in seeing the "priceless" in the act of *giving.* Especially gifts that don't cost a penny.

However, once we experience the abundant joy we receive from your acts of thoughtful giving, we'll be yours for life and will let you know how appreciative we truly are.

This simple strategy will enrich all your relationships . . . guaranteed.

> You just have to take the risk.
> Jump off the giving edge.
> Take the plunge. Take that swing.
> Reach for the hoop. Go for it.

You've got NOTHING to lose.

Myth:
Getting the size right and
getting the right size.
Fact:
In your dreams.
It's close to impossible!
But this chapter will help you
get it right more of the time.

The number of high stress groans and fierce
exclamations like "I'm never buying clothes as
a gift again!" rank FIRST, and far ahead of any
other gift giving stress producers on the list.

Ann Hult Crowell

Sizing Up Your Recipient.

Proceed With Caution!!
It's A Minefield In Motion.

The size possibilities are endless — like finding the right size in a field of booby traps (no pun intended) just waiting to blow your idea of "the right size" to smithereens.

Fortunately, with the *"Wrap It Up!"* time-tested and proven ways to get and apply sizes you're more likely to pick the correct size for your Succulent Sweetheart on the first try. The strategy is simple and repeatable.

If you're one of those rare Size-Wise-Wonder-Guys who already have this size thing down to a science, give this 3-minutes of your time just to make sure you maintain your consistent successes in this elusive, ever-changing size arena.

PSST: Your own experiences in this area, and your creative ideas are indeed welcome. We'll respect your privacy. Please share at *www.wrapitupbooks.com*

6 Areas Where Size Is Certain . . . Without Measuring

Fingers. They beg for rings to enhance those graceful hands that provide a gentle touch on your cheek or light massage on the back of your neck.

Ears. The perfect perch for baubles, dangles and precious stones. An invitation for you to nibble.

Neck. Always happy decorated.

Nose. I smell a diamond.

Belly Buttons. Watch out. These piercings twinkle and shine and are sought after by teens, tweens, babes and baby boomers.
PSSST: Don't leave out Granny — 'bout time she had something other than slippers and blankets.

Toes. Tasty toe rings. Ankle bracelets with bangles and jangles. Strappy and seductive sandals with skinny 4″ heels — so ready to go dancing. Serious boots for happy hiking to high places.

And Where Else Do You Suppose?
Go ahead. Get creative.

5 Reasons It's So Difficult To Nail Down The Right Size

1. **Sizes differ from one <u>outfit/style</u> to another.**
   Even if it's from the <u>same manufacturer</u>. Has to do with the style. Pants or skirts. Tailored or loose. Cocktail dresses or sporty beach shifts.

2. **Your Beloved's <u>body type</u> influences size.**
   For example, if she's amply endowed (has big boobs) and flat butt you're in for two sizes. Larger for the top, smaller for the bottom. And vice-versa — For a dress or one-piece item, go for the middle, hope for the best.

3. **Sizes change from one designer or manufacturer to another.**
   An 8 from one is <u>not</u> always an 8 from another Whether it's affordable, mid-priced, or expensive.

4. **A <u>0</u> can also be an <u>8</u>! Confused yet?**
   A size 0 (yup, that's a zero) from one designer or manufacturer can fit a 4, 6 or 8 from another. If it's a loose jacket, a 10 often can wear a 0. Fun eh?

5. **Manufacturers change sizes from one season to another. Why?**
   Vanity? Smaller <u>sounds</u> better! We like that.

9 Size Facts You Gotta Have

1. Height   ____

2. Weight   ____
   Yeah Right. In your dreams.

3. Bust/Chest   ____

4. Under Bust
   Aka Rib Cage   ____

5. Waist   ____

6. Hips   __

7. Wrist   ____

8. Ring Finger   ____

9. Shoe Length   ____   Width   ____

VIP: Forget "One Size Fits All." <u>It doesn't!</u>

PSST: Record all information immediately in your *Pocket Informant©*, the *"Wrap It Up!"* book or both.

Size Combo's You Need For:

1. **Dresses**
   Height ___ Bust ___ Waist ___ Hips ___

2. **Shirts**
   Bust/Chest ____ Sleeve Length ___

3. **Fitted Tops**
   Bust ___ Under Bust ___ Waist ___

4. **Skirts**
   Waist ___ Hips ___

5. **Pants**
   Waist ___ Hips ___

6. **Jackets**
   Bust/Chest ___ Waist ___ Hips ___

7. **Sports Wear**
   Bust/Chest ___ Waist ___ Hips ___

8. **Sport/Casual Shoes**
   Standard Shoe Size Length ___ Width ___

9. **Dressy Shoes**
   Standard Shoe Size Length ___ Width ___
   See Outta Sight Insights© for Twinkle Toes ideas

10. **Intimate Apparel**
    Bust ___ Waist ___ Hips ___

3 Ways To Get Size Information

1. Ask your Inspiring One directly
Ask simple questions. Confirm if you can.
PSST: Recipients often *distort* this information.
   "I'll be a size ____ when I go on that diet."

2. Get the information *On-The-Sly*
Easiest if you're cohabitating. Wait till they go for
   their AM jog, to work, grocery shopping or
   leave for a business trip.
Head for dresser drawers and the closet.
Look for size labels in waistbands, necklines, side
   seams, inside or bottom of shoes. Put it back
   like you found it. Grab a ring — get it sized at
   the jeweler. Sneak it back promptly.

3. What to do when 1 or 2 fail
Pick up the phone and call their best friend, sister
   or mother. Swear them to secrecy.

Don't worry if they "tell." You'll get big points
   for your thoughtfulness and it's good for your
   reputation.

VIP: Record all information immediately in
   this book or your *Pocket Informant©*

The 5 Rules Of Successful Size Sleuthing

RULE 1 — Have ALL data gathering materials ready

RULE 2 — Use a tailor's measuring tape. NOT to be confused with your metal carpenter's tape.

RULE 3 — Get all information FAR in advance of any event. ASAP.

RULE 4 — Get ALL sizes at one time — if possible.

RULE 5 — Enter the data in PENCIL in your *Pocket Informant©* or in *"Wrap It Up!"*

REMEMBER — This is NOT a conversation with your doctor or periodontist. It's your:

Beloved	Significant Other
Leading Lady	Intuitive Other
Object Of Your Affection	Close Friend
Potential Love Candidate	Love of Your Life

Outta Sight Insights©
Discover What Makes Us Tick.

The 5 Rules Of Size Sleuthing
E X P A N D E D

RULE 1 — Have all data gathering materials ready

- Two <u>Pencils</u> — Never write sizes in ink
- Your copy of *"Wrap It Up!"* where you'll find a list of the "measurable data" you need
- Your *Pocket Informant©* so you can have the critical data available on short notice — like in your wallet

RULE 2 — Use a standard tape measure. NOT to be confused with your metal carpenter's retractable tape.

- Available at most supermarkets or combo pharmacy/general store. Ask for a "Tape Measure."

RULE 3 — Three Important NEVER's

It's NEVER a good idea to pop the size question until the two of you have established a resonable level of mutual interest . . . then ask basic questions gracefully.
- After you've asked her out for a while
- The moment you start serious courting

NEVER start your Q&A just two or three days before a gift-giving event.

Your Special One wants to believe that you've spent weeks, many weeks, planning this thoughtful treasure. What?! You haven't started? Get busy, guy. The happy ending of your gift giving may depend on it.

NEVER, NEVER look surprised, gasp, sigh or exude any kind of discourteous grunt or body movement that might be interpreted in the wrong way. That is, anything other than normal behavior. Simply "ASK, SMILE AND ENTER THE DATA."

RULE 4 — Get ALL sizes at one time — if possible.

Unless, of course, this is a very new and/or slow get-acquainted time. In those cases such questions can give the impression you're keeping score to see how New Succulent stacks up against Former Tenderheart. You <u>don't</u> want to raise that flag.

- Get the vital statistics at one sitting
- Over a favorite soft drink or glass of wine
- With eye contact, smiles and little snuggles

This is a loving inquiry and you'll both enjoy the fruits of the effort. Really.

RULE 5 — Enter the data in PENCIL

- Use the pages in this chapter to enter data
- Record it in your *Pocket Informant© too.* In pencil
- Enter it on "My Gift Guide" at <u>www.wrapitupbookss.com</u>
- Put the data in your computer and make a wallet copy
- Keep your work sheets locked in a afe/private place

3 VIP Girl-Things To Remember

So You Don't Accidentally Sabotage
The Size Search Process.

1. When asked our size we often lie. *"Maybe I can squeeze into an 8 after all."*
   My heart goes out to you, guys. You're brave to even tackle this minefield! Stick around. The end results are worth the effort.

2. We "hide" or "remove" size tags
   because they always sound much toooo big. Or bigger than we'll be when we start on that diet.

   When shopping alone, we *ignore* the size on the label. If it fits, we rip out the size ID and wear the outfit. With <u>nothing</u> but our glorious smile.

3. We're easily bored. Change our minds and our sizes often.
   Just about the time you've got us figured out we're off in another style and size direction. Wears us out too. Still, shopping is sooooo fun. Well, for us it is.

GOOD NEWS! BAD NEWS!

GOOD: And You Thought Size Was Just *Your* Problem?

BAD: Size Is Gnarly For Us, Too!

Every man I've talked to on the size topic says, "The size thing's a real problem. REALLY frustrating." Then his eyes glaze over and he mumbles, "I NEVER get it right! I need HELP!"

Please know that GIRLS IN PARTICULAR HAVE THE SAME PROBLEM! We need HELP, too.

We're NOT frustrated because you don't buy us the right size. We're frustrated because it's not easy for US to find the right size either.

"No way," you say, "That's NOT possible."

Well, it IS true. And get this! We're there in the flesh to try things on!

We are all born for love.
It is the principle of existence
And its only end.

Benjamin Disralei

The *"Wrap It Up!"*© WRAP UP

It's All About Giving Plus
The Gratitude, Affection and Warmth
You'll Receive In Return.

I promised a gift for YOU Gentlemen that would change your experience and life with the objects of your affection.

All of them.
For the better.
Forever.

It might be a 52-year marriage partner, a new attraction, a mother, daughter, sister, cousin, grandma, Auntie Mame, a friend, co-workers. It's a long list.

At the very least your giving nature will dramatically reduce complaining (AKA bitching) and the bitter drip-method of not-so-kind reminders that, "You let someone down — again!"

On the up side, you will now be the frequent recipient of gratitude and other caring expressions (personal gifts back to you) that will leave you gasping for air, wanting more and being happier than you ever imagined possible.

You've learned all you need to know about what to give, when, where, what size, how to wrap it, what to say on the card, and how to present it.

You're now ready and willing to receive your "rewards" in return.

After all, if credit card companies can give you a "reward" for spending money with <u>them</u>, imagine the potential of getting rewards from your creative and luscious recipients because you lavished on <u>them</u> — without your credit card.

With your imagination and a few hints from *"Wrap It Up!"*, you can uncover a whole new realm of delectable life experiences — that won't interfere with your most favorite "game."

You're going to enjoy experiences that have the potential of transforming all your relationships with your recipients from:
    Ho-hum to Happy
    Routine to Remarkable
    Bland to Bliss

The real secret is that *"Wrap It Up!"* isn't about the gifts. It's about the *giving*.

The stuff that doesn't cost a penny.
Acts of giving that let us others know you cherish
them. Giving generously of your thoughtfulness, caring, attention, the promises you keep and the little
acts of kindness you deliver on a frequent basis.

It's about unexpected delights. The sum total of
which add up to enriching your relationships and
warming the hearts, minds, and bodies of all. For a
long time to come.

So, hang in there. You have discovered plenty of simple recipes in this book that all deliver one reward in
common.

Bliss.

Sheer. Dazzling. Bliss.

Go forward Guys, Gentlemen and Young-Men-At-
Heart. Have fun, be happy and let your heart call the
shots.

If I have seen further it is by
standing on the shoulders of giants.

Isaac Newton

Special Thanks

As part of a Vision Process I was asked to write down ten of the most important things I had done in my life, how I went about doing them and did I have help. After writing the list and starting to answer the "how" and "who helped" questions I realized, the answers were the same. It was the "who helped" that took my breath away. My helpers were giants of talent, inspiration, untiring support and excitement that gave wings to the *ten things*, and the wind under them so they could fly to amazing heights.

Undertaking *"Wrap It Up!"*© brought giants, heroes and heroines into my life and I thank them copiously for their help in writing this book and for sharing their personal brand of input. They must begin with my former husband, Tony Crowell, whose gift-giving skills provided endless delight to me and were the envy of all my girlfriends. His skills begged to be shared.

For those whose encouragement and steadfast support inspired me to actually start writing this book, and at whose insistence and confidence-giving counsel made sure I finished, I am eternally grateful for my heroes; Vance Caesar, Terry Crowther, Jerry Downs, Jeff Clark, Richard Henson and Heath Celestin — the men who have shared their invaluable insights, intellect and who revealed their innermost gift-buying frustrations. Who added their individual spice and creative ideas to the mix. And who collectively insisted I keep it "short, useful and to the point!"

To amazing heroines, my smart, wise and beautiful girlfriends, who bless my life daily and whose herding instincts kept me focused — no small challenge — I give abundant thanks: Pam Bennett, Frumi Barr, Linda Fini, Mary Smith, Julie Corman, Peggy Coldwater Clay, Betsy Sanders, Donna Haskell, Elkie Muller, Darian Larsen and Beth Lance.

For their patience, sense of humor, always cheerful working style and rocket-speed turn-around times my Sheridan Books team Polly Lawrence, Kathy Brown, Jean Schroeder and the press group, deserve a standing ovation.

To Roger Corman, who crowned the effort, I shall be eternally grateful for his friendship, sharing his thoughts on giving and gifts, and comments about this book.

Contact & Ordering Information

Please visit
www.WrapItUpBooks.com

We add new services regularly to help you
get it right all the time.

Register for our FREE "Wrap It Up!"
reminder service and the FREE monthly
"Wrap It Up!"© *e-Zine* featuring:
What's Hot and What's Not© gift ideas,
Outta Sight Insights©.

Order The *Pocket Informant*©

Buy additional copies of *"Wrap It Up!"*

Check speaking and seminar schedules and
other related events.

Go to
www.WrapItUpBooks.com

Special Buying Notes

Special Buying Notes

Special Buying Notes